W O R D S
T H
A A
K P
E

Poetry by
Ashley Roncaglione

Words Take Shape

DARK THIRTY POETRY PUBLISHING

ISBN: 978-1-0685766-3-8

Roncaglione, Ashley

First edition

Artwork by Ellie H Artwork

DTPP34

DARK
THIRTY
POETRY
PUBLISHING

Try as I might, the sounds never escape.
If I write this all down, then my words take shape.

For KK.

Table of Contents

Hivemind

I often wonder if you think of me
in the exact moments that I think of you.
Do your lips tingle as I drink my morning coffee?
I imagine that you hum along, wherever you are,
when I'm singing in my car.
The tag in my shirt is bothersome.
Do you lift your hand to scratch your neck?
When my fingers rest against my thighs,
is my warmth radiating in your belly?
And now, as I go to bed,
do you see me behind closed eyes?
If so, then we're both dreaming
the same violent dreams.

zoomorph

swathed in
the white glow
and drunk on the night air
you and me standing in
the middle of Terry Road
howling at the moon and
erupting in violent laughter
as the coyotes answered our feral calls
communal echoes of the bloodlust
a recognition of the hunger
I can’t say for certain that
that we didn’t return home
on all fours

the outlier

don't you feel it there
it's close but out of reach yet
a black silhouette against a night sky
breath is fogging the glass
but I am beginning to make out the shape
a hunger unrelenting
my
knees
begin
to
falter

Sap

Tapping into your subconscious
my body   the spile

Bone Memory

if you were to cut me open
you wouldn't find

twenty-two feet of intestines
or quivering organs softly padded in
their visceral fat

instead— a torsional rope of
unspoken words

strangulated

gasping

ischemic

a life ingrown, pustulating on bone

Lumina

intra-cloud flashes
        lightning that almost
touches the ground
            shadow illuminated across
a violent sky
              you should see my words almost
leaving my mouth
                              sparks of light dancing
behind my lips almost
                            reaching your ears
I guess that makes me
              intra-communicational
always an almost
                  almost
but not quite

night palette

color in hidden shadow is found
silken sapphire and softened shades
of silence shrouded in sovereign sound
last light surrounds as whispers fade

organs

love is violence in disguise
she grips, tears, bleeds, consumes
living and breathing in obsession

and if she dies
her remains still pulse in their finality
just as the snake still writhes
with a severed head

love is violence—her blade a scythe

oversaturation

to feel
to learn
to taste
to yearn
to see
to breathe
to trust
to burn
to behold
this beauty
to reach
to touch
to exist
with pain
it's all
too much

nearly> <touching

how many electrons span our distance
miles apart yet nearly touching
ions colliding and pressure building
i can carve it with the edge of my hand
we both can sense every impending
lightning strike between us
that finds its release on the hungry ground
so tell me then how many words
left unspoken can one possibly withstand
with crackling air and static lungs
my hitching breath and crumbling resolve
when your fingertips finally reach through
the atmospheric currents and settle where they land
will my skin show the electrical burns as evidence
that your touch was really there

black noise

it’s quiet here
peace should find me
but I can’t stop reaching for
the lull of bitter sonance

in dreams

clenched jaws and men in masks
hands bound with rope
words so close I feel the spittle
no convincing can temper
I feel it there
the warmth
r a d i a t e s

covalent b o n d s

if my body w e r e   t o
disassemble w h e r   e
cells no longer a d h e r   e
to one a n o t h   e   r
my violent a t o m s
splitting a p a r t   a n d
dispelling th e i r   o w   n
orbital   s h e l   l   s

would I   evapor a t e   l   i   k   e
the sweat from   a   p o r e
my fingers   be c o m i   n   g
the steam ri s i   n   g
off of damp e n e d   s k   i   n
my vapor   colle c t i n g   a n d
condensing in atmo s p h   e   r   e
as   c l o   u   d   s

would I then ref l   e   c   t   t   h   e
secret prism   o f   li g   h   t
my particles in ref r a c   t   i   o   n
of the glorious spe c t   r   u   m
perhaps this i s   h o w   w   e
behold t h e   d i v i   n   e
surrendering t h e   b o   d   y
the dissociation o f   s e l   f

Breach

Is my body really my own?
I'm not so sure anymore
My thoughts of you feel intrusive
A violation
I should have agency here
But you are seeping into spaces
That were once airtight

Pyrexia

in the farthest synapse
axonal shifts and diffuse feeling
the sounds of corpus callosum
sparks
between dimensional spaces
glasgow can't measure
three point three isn't that heavy
pulse
fever dream deepening
lacquer eyes give witness
do echoes drift on currents?
wake

HERM SPRENGER

my grief resists me
such a brittle companion
with vitreous shards
no longer do we fit together
as the interlacing of fingers
so delicately it once
sank into my contours
now it greets me
with a biting disdain
a barbed hook
in opposition of
struggling flesh

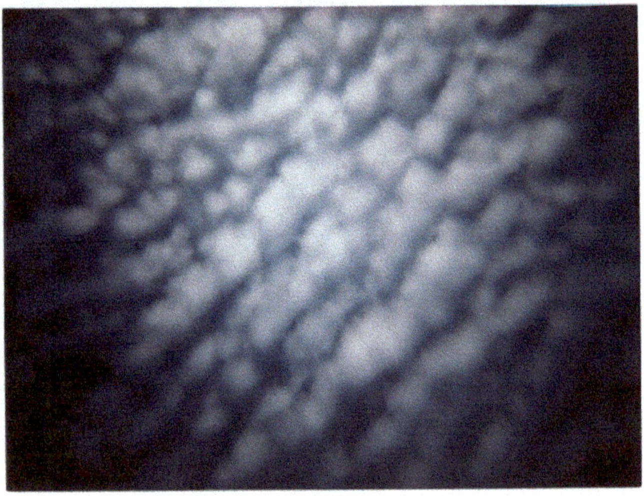

Rootbound

Something grows beneath the surface
A slow expanse
A spatial release
The seed seeks more ground
That no amount can satiate

The Sower's trowel is lacking purchase
The roots are bound
Dendritic increase
Only starlight lends to soil quenched
As branches bend under heavy weight

Shovel

How long will I dig
This abysmal hole
Hands blistered
Digits withered
Every increment
My detriment
I reach for the wind but the
Weather is too inclement

Can't bargain with god
An insurmountable toll
Traps triggered
Sticks splintered
Grave imminent
Death ambivalent
I am Adam incarnate
My flesh is imprisonment

schist

sandstone lime
beneath my feet I greet the edge
at Yavapai eyes so eager lay witness to the
interlacing fingers of light and shadow
air from humble lungs is stolen as the canyons
breathe a rock that seethes erupts hues so golden
fire's lingering mist a holy shroud for glowing schist
unworthy tears cloud my vision as I am told
a beauty so violent is too sacred to behold

Trash Day

Friday is trash collection day
I open the lid to
pull the drawstring
A band-aid or a q-tip sits
always at the bottom
under the trash bag
I am just too lazy
to reach inside and
remove it
If it were inside
the trash bag
maybe it would
decompose faster
Google says
5 months for a q-tip and
centuries for a band-aid
Still, it remains
under the trash bag
stuck to the bottom
I guess that means
that some things
disposed of
never make it to the
landfill—
they stay with you

p a r t i c u l a t e

t h e r e i s a serenity in the br e a k d o w n
u n r a v e l ling, disassembling, crum b l i n g
d i s solving—the way edges begin to so f t e n
g i v i n g way and losing shape—h o w t h e
p i e c e s fall, scatter, and litter the f l o o r
l i k e t h e d u s t o f
f l u o r e s c e n t b u l b s
s o m e s m e r i z e d i w a s
b y t h e w a y

t h e p a r t i c l e s

c a t c h t h e l i g h t

t h a t i a l m o s t d i d

n o t n o t i c e t h e

d i s a p p e a r a n c e

o f y o u r f o r m

a l l t o g e t h e r

windswept

she was
his mother
her translucence
is spreading
and idly he sits
in the chair while
I auscultate for sounds
a final whisper uttered
through her windswept tree
and there is too long of a pause
with the anticipation between
our unspoken words
eternity is now imminent
so loud it seems
in the absence of beats
will her music drift as
her mouth sighs its last secret
my ears the sole recipient
of such beautiful chords
soon her body will be buried
last breath is too heavy
for lungs to hold

asymmetry

where did
you go?
did you not
hear
my cries
for help
through the echoes
of the waves?
I thought I saw
a bird
fall from
the sky and I wanted
to tell you
how it feels
like the
universe is
speaking to me

how I'm
always
searching the
water for my own face
peering back
but it remains
unseen
isn't a reflection
supposed to be
a perfect match?
my inkblot
in the mirror
yet the symmetry
is not there
you do not answer me
so I guess it's time
I remove
the feathers
from my hair

drip

.
.
. .
water
in veins
my water
s t a i n s
water between
r i b s
we bellow
in caves
. .
.
. .
drips
fr o m
l i p s
f l o o d i n g
o u r h i p s
fire in depths
n o w a t e r
can save
. .
.
.

sediment

theweightisso whatwordswillfilterthrough unyieldinglips
evenwastewaterbecomes asitseepsthroughthegravelandmud
this canonlycontainsomuchuntil seamseventuallypullandtear
asmysyllablestake andsoftlyfalltothegroundwill collecteach
oneandgently thesounds theirmeaningburrowsinsideyou
aslowdripa gripeveryunspokenwordwithacyclicaldeath
theweightissocrushingwhat willfilterthroughmyhesitantbreath

crushing my
purified
body the
shape you
cradle before
strangulating
words

Supplication

My pulse is thrumming
The hum of the drones
Will too soon cease
Isn't God found in our
Empty spaces just as
The fog settles in the
Belly of the valley
I long for reprieve
Release me I beg you
All marks leave traces
I expel these words
Lest they carry weightless
My suspended breath
Almost as agonizing as
An ellipsis at the end of
Every perilous sentence...

se ver

no longer do they linger
I severed the red cord of my
around little fingers my wounds
the great exodus the tissue
from my life is it granular
I can see it no suturing can
in pictures bridge this distance
the slow dehiscence in diameter
i t c h is this what happens when
the truth becomes avascular

devil's mark

sin translates
to missing
the mark
missing the
mark requires first
aiming at the target
what is it called when
you have no aim?
as a child
I a m aimless
and therefore
b l a m e l e s s

fracture

I broke what we had. / /A fractured surface no longer smooth.
The pieces catch the/ /light now in the most unusual of ways.
Their shadows play \ \in a kaleidoscopic dance on the ceiling.
There is no escaping \ \this prognosis. This incurable disease.
You're now my host / / and I'm the dreaded cancer diagnosis.

edge

it
always
feels
like
get I'm
ready losing
now grip
I'm
if on
I the
pull cusp
you
over
from the
thirsty edge
lips with
I me
these may
slippery just
words let

f
a
l
l

stain

You're on my garments
Lingering in my hair
Upholstery
Wrapped around my pulse points
The sour on my tongue
Noticeable on the exhale
It excites me
The places you have touched
The places you haven't left

there are two butterflies outside my window

the iridescence on the scales
a fine dust that collects on eager fingertips
I was once that child
not yet knowing the art of handling delicate wings
no, they do not pass through life unscathed
the evidence is revealed on the edges that fray
and they still take flight in defiance
seemingly held by the wind's embrace
a life captured in only 2 short weeks
my hands have also eroded with time
the pain in this brevity
is far too beautiful to be measured

what is it like

to be in
the midst of
requited love where
conditions have no
purchase on its
hallowed ground

to see the
life it gives
the blood it pours
it breathes with
lungs it touches
the source

has the eye seen
or the ear heard
has the mind learnt
or the heart felt
this inexorable pause
demanding to be held

semi-permanance

```
t t o o e i t m w l t m w s a
h r f u x s h o e i h o e l w
e u   r i   e r   n e r   i a
  t     s     e   g   e   p y
  h     t         e
        e         r
        n
        c
        e
```

utterance

on silent seas
with windless sails
and leafless trees
no shade to veil
a whispered word
on absent breath
a voice unheard
it speaks of death

God is a poet

Their words cast shadows against the sinking sun
And are whispered into the laughter among trees
The language of God is in the kiss of another
Traces of ink found in the breath against bare skin
Birds of one accord recite supernal scripture
From verses inscribed in the melting of the sky
God is a poet and their pen writes wonders
And in lust of Nature they command all to read

Acknowledgments

I'd like to give my sincerest thanks to my wonderful publisher and editor, Adam--the genius behind Dark Thirty Poetry Publishing. Also, I would like express gratitude to Carolina Muse & Literary Arts Magazine, Curio Cabinet Magazine, Mulberry Literary, and Same Faces Collective for publishing the following poems:

Carolina Muse & Literary Arts Magazine - "Oversaturation" and "Asymmetry"

Curio Cabinet Magazine – "Covalent Bonds"

Mulberry Literary – "Particulate," "Nearly Touching," and "Herm Sprenger"

Same Faces Collective – "Schist"

Ashley Roncaglione is a registered nurse living in Durham, North Carolina. She is a beekeeper, multimedia artist, poet, and animal lover. Themes on mental health, trauma, and the human experience are sources of inspiration for her writing. She has been featured in several publications by Dark Thirty Poetry Publishing as well as Carolina Muse Literary & Arts Magazine. This is her second collection of poetry.

RELEASED BY DARK THIRTY POETRY

ANTHOLOGY ONE
THIS ISN'T WHY WE'RE HERE
MORTAL BEINGS
POEMS THAT WERE WRITTEN ON TRAINS BUT WEREN'T WRITTEN ABOUT TRAINS
CLOSING SHIFT DREAMS
DESIRE
ANIMATE
THESEUS AND I
I DON'T HAVE THE WORDS FOR THIS
CONVERSATIONS BETWEEN THE SUN AND THE MOON
SLUTPOP
JADED
I'VE BIRTHED AN IDEA OF YOU
BRUISES
CITY GOTHIC
LONG DIVISION
SAY HER NAME
LUMIN
VESTIGES
FALLING IN LOVE LOST
JUGGERNAUT
STIRRING TO LIFE
FORGOTTEN FRAGMENTS OF TIME
THIS BOOK IS NOT ABOUT JAPAN
BEYOND THE DOORS OF A LAST BREATH
CORPORATE
JANE F*CKING EYRE
THE SNAKE EATS ITSELF
THE MOON AND HER CRATERS
NOCTURNAL
BREWING ANXIETEA
FLAT FRONT
ARE YOU HAVING A GOOD TIME YET?
WORDS TAKE SHAPE

www.ingramcontent.com/pod-product-compliance
Lightning Source LLC
Chambersburg PA
CBHW070631050426
42450CB00011B/3161
9781068576638